A SWIFT RIVER ANTHOLOGY

A Swift River Anthology

Dorothy Johnson

illustrations and cover design by
C. V. Smith

Haley's
Athol, Massachusetts

Haley's
488 South Main Street
Athol, MA 01331
haley.antique@verizon.net
800.215.8805

International Standard Book Number: 978-1-884540-33-2
Library of Congress Catalogue Number: 2011926772

All the characters in this book have no existence outside the
imagination of the author and have no relation whatsoever to
anyone bearing the same name or names. They are not even
distantly inspired by any individual known or unknown to the
author, and all incidents are pure invention.

Cover design and illustrations by C. V. Smith.

Special thanks to Menotomy Maps, www.menotomymaps.com,
for permission to reproduce the cover map and to Mary-Ann
DeVita Palmieri and Linda Overing.

To the memory of my parents
Ted and Edith Johnson
who lived in Smith's Village before I was born
and, of course,
to the memory of Doris

Contents

Illustrations by C. V. Smith accompany each of the entries.

PROLOGUE

The concept of individual ownership of homes and land is basic to this country's ideals, so it is more than upsetting when a government decides that land can be taken by eminent domain for the good of its citizens. In 1926, the Commonwealth of Massachusetts passed a law taking the land in the Swift River Valley to create a reservoir for eastern Massachusetts.

People had settled the land, farmed, schooled their children, built houses of worship, and built up towns for generations—the taking of their land must have been cataclysmic. While some may have been relieved to be free of the relentless work of a hard-scrabble farm, most were devastated and angry. They fought it for as long as they could, but in the end, they had to move. The work began in 1926, and the reservoir was completed in 1938.

The towns of Dana, Enfield, Greenwich, and Prescott emptied slowly and carefully. All the inhabitants moved with their possessions, and their houses were sold, razed, or burned to the ground. It was not uncommon to see trucks slowly carrying houses along the valley's roads. Trees were cut, and the hills along the river looked barren. Men had come in from Boston to cut trees and work in the valley. People said that Mayor Curley emptied out the Boston streets to provide workers, and valley folk called them "woodpeckers." The valley must have looked like a war-torn countryside as it was emptied of everything people had known in the four towns. Even cemeteries were not left untouched. Coffins were disinterred and re-buried in the then new Quabbin Park Cemetery across from the dam. While it must have seemed raw when that work was first done, now the cemetery is a quiet, restful place.

I visited it in the summer of 2010 and walked along the roads looking at the gravestones that had once stood in other places. There were new stones, too, as family members joined those who had gone before. You had to think of the individuals who were buried there. There was no way around it, and that brought to mind Edgar Lee Masters's 1915 *Spoon River Anthology*. Masters's work compiled poems written about people buried in an Illinois graveyard. It seemed only natural to consider a Swift River anthology by borrowing the title, format, and notion that there are voices in a graveyard.

The Quabbin area is rich in history and rich in actual character, but I decided that the people in my anthology would be created in my imagination. It would be wrong to ascribe words and feelings to real people because I would have no way to know them. Instead, I tell stories. After all, I was raised on stories.

Both my parents were story tellers. Most of my mother's stories were about her family, her aunts and cousins, and the neighbors in Holyoke during the early years of the twentieth century. My father's were often about the Swift River Valley. When my parents married in 1926, they lived on a farm in Belchertown. The farm got burned out, so they rented a different farm in Smith's Village, a part of Enfield. The original owners had already left the valley, so my parents were able to rent from the Metropolitan District Commission—charged with over-seeing the Quabbin project and all that it entailed—for a nominal fee. They had that place sometime between 1928 and the end of 1932. My brother and sister both lived there, but by the time I was born in 1933, my parents had bought a small bungalow in South Hadley.

My parents were a little vague about exact dates precisely be-cause they both were story tellers. Actual details were irrelevant. My mother did claim that her first vote was cast in Enfield. She was about to be twenty-one and both my grandfathers were ardent Re-publicans. They nagged her incessantly, so when election day came in Enfield, she cast her vote defiantly. She claimed to be the first Socialist vote in town. Norman Thomas was her candidate.

They loved old things, and the house where I grew up held a sense of the past. My parents ended up as antique dealers. We had portraits of other people's ancestors on our walls. Most of the furni-ture was old and for sale, so our "past" kept changing. Sometimes we would have breakfast sitting on a set of Hitchcock chairs and supper on mismatched Windsors. Between the antique business and my parents' story telling I grew up with an appreciation for old things and old stories.

I now live in an old house in New Salem. You couldn't live here without the Quabbin Reservoir becoming part of your conscious-ness. Main Street comes to a dead end because of the reservoir. Route 202 neatly divides the town. The center of town where the common is and where town buildings are is on one side of the interstate road with a limited number of residences. The other side has more houses and more land available for development. The Swift River Historical Society, housing a vast collection of memorabilia from Quabbin towns, is on Elm Street on the North New Salem side. Of course, probably every town surrounding the reservoir keeps the ghosts of the towns that used to be. As I grow older, I have become more aware of them.

So how could I not tell stories? Over the years, most of my story telling has been in the form of plays, and in the last twenty-five or thirty years the plays have been New England stories. The 1794 Meetinghouse, just two doors down from my address, has produced many of my plays. I keep an open-door policy on casting so that anyone who wants to be in the play can have a part. I write for those self-identified actors. Over the years, many of the same people come back, and new people arrive. We end up with a large cast, and I am obliged to write a part for each.

Plays are about people, naturally. From *Oedipus Rex* through *The Homestead*, each play is about human beings and their actions. Each character has something to say, and it is something that *only* he or she can say if it is to ring true. A playwright then must be able to stand aside and let that character speak in his own voice. For me, that is what *A Swift River Anthology* is: people who must give voice to what they feel. I hope I have stood aside sufficiently so that they do speak for themselves.

Opening Words

Where are the towns
where people lived and died?
Where are those they left behind?
Are they sleeping in this place?
Where is Etta who could talk
the wings off a hummingbird?
Or Burt who painted all those paintings of
   his home place?
Or Donald who wrote a book
about the Lost Valley?
Are they sleeping in this place
or are they sleeping under other quiet stones
in other quiet places?
Are they all content now and at rest?
What of the others who died
after the waters covered their birthplaces?
Do they come here
to join the folks who have already
gone to glory and sleep here?
Are they all at rest?
But do some from the Valley ever come awake
to see the waters shimmer in the sun?
To watch the birds, the deer,
the people fishing over their towns?
Do they ever see the eagles?
Or are they complete, content to rest forever
sleeping in this place?

Mary Elizabeth Carver
1851-1906

Mary Elizabeth Carver

1851-1906

I loved my life,
every hour, every day, every year.
I had the love of a good man
who shared his thoughts with me.
Our children grew strong and tall,
even Eddie who was sickly as a child.
We worked hard and found joy in it.
I think I was one of the lucky ones.

Billy Reardon
1850-1916

Billy Reardon

1850-1916

I went to Chancellorsville,
holding the flag
as long as I could
till Johnny Reb knocked it out of my hands
and his horse trampled me.
I came home no hero,
no medals, and no left leg.
I shaped a peg for me to stand on
and took up a trade.
I built houses and barns
to stand in Prescott
as long as they could.

Nora Barton
1764-1807

Nora Barton

1764-1807

Rough hands moved me here
and jostled my bones.
Life was hard enough
that I was glad to come to rest
in Dana where all was quiet.

Why did they move me
to this place?

George Ransom Olds, Jr.
1893-1918

George Ransom Olds, Jr.

1893-1918

I was raised in Enfield
and expected to spend all my days there
working on the family farm.
But the government said I was needed elsewhere,
and they sent me to France
on a ship with men singing "Over There."
Then they sent me back
with failing lungs.
I killed no Germans,
and I didn't die in battle.
Yet the war over there killed me over here.

George Ransom Olds, Sr.
1875-1926

George Ransom Olds, Sr.

1875-1926

I married Geneva Scott
when we were young.
We hoped for a big family,
but the wife got sick giving birth
to George, Junior.
We raised him to be a man
and built up the farm for him,
but it wasn't to be.
It broke Geneva's heart
to see him go like that.
Now they want my farm.
Hasn't the government taken enough from me?

Laura Bascomb White
1856-1933

Laura Bascomb White

1856-1933

For years I taught school in Greenwich
and thought I'd never marry.
Then Lester White wooed me quietly
when I was almost thirty.
He was known to be a quiet man.
And after he said, "I do,"
I found he had no other words.
We ate our meals in silence.
Sometimes I'd ache for the sound of a voice.
Finally the children came
one after another,
and voices filled the house.
He died one afternoon
when I was on a picnic with the children.
Even on that day, he couldn't say he was sick.
After the funeral we hardly noticed
he wasn't there any more.

Barnaby Cooper
1710-1792

Barnaby Cooper

1710-1792

I don't remember the war.
Perhaps I went.
I do remember that when the war was ended,
life was harder.
Prices went up, and taxes soared.
Daniel Shays came to Enfield Common
looking for men to fight the new government.
I couldn't see that fighting fixed anything,
so I stayed home.
It was enough for me
to tend my cows and shear my sheep.

Rebecca Cooper Crowe
1735-1770

Rebecca Cooper Crowe

1735-1770

Levi Crowe and I were married in 1751.
I knew about housekeeping
because my mother needed my help when I was young.
I could fetch water, tend the cows, make porridge,
and shoot a musket too,
but all I knew about marriage
I learned from watching the bull
and the ram with their females.
I died when little Ethan was born,
and another woman raised him and the girls
along with their own.
Levi's next wife is buried here, too,
close to his third. He lived to be eighty.
I'm told he bragged about his exploits
in the war, but who tended his house
when he was away?

George Washington Crowe
1780-1842

George Washington Crowe

1780-1842

My father seemed old to me always.
I lived in Greenwich
with my half brothers and sisters
who remained at home until marriage.
My father outlived my mother,
and I looked after him.
We got along, and I knew
no other family.

Wingo Beard
1790-1883

Wingo Beard

1790-1883

I built my own house with barn attached.
The barn was bigger, of course.
Though my wife complained,
I knew what was important.
Winter times you could go from house to barn
without shoveling snow.
The orchard provided apples,
and the meadow had good hay.
My cows were well fed
and provided the good rich milk.
What was there to complain about?

Dolley Flynn Madison
1860-1910

Dolley Flynn Madison

1860-1910

I never should have married him.
I could have gone through life as Dolley Flynn
or Dolley anything else,
and I'd have missed the jokes.
But then I'd have missed Leander.
He was worth it, but let me tell you,
a joke about a name is never new.

Laurentia Stipple
1878-1917

Laurentia Stipple

1878-1917

My needlework was my pride.
Careful small stitches, precise straight lines.
Every sheet, every pillowslip and tablecloth.
I placed each one in my hope chest neatly.
It was maple and made to my specifications.
Then I waited and waited.
When no one came, finally
I took the linen
and all the fine white clothes
out of the hope chest and put them neatly on the floor.
Then I opened the empty chest, climbed in,
and heard the lid slam shut.
Whatever hope I had was gone.

Warren Webster Whitcomb

1896-1945

Warren Webster Whitcomb

1896-1945

Nobody knew my secret.
They wished and they envied,
but they never learned
how I succeeded.
They could have asked.
When the sun was rising in the west,
I might have told them.
The discerning few who understood
knew how hard I worked.
If my neighbors with their scrawny imaginations
had watched me rather than wishing
for a magic wand to bring them happiness,
they might have understood.
Honest hard work is happiness in itself.

Edwina L. Pearl
1852-1920

Edwina L. Pearl

1852-1920

I was called the cat lady of Dana.
There were cats in my house,
in my barn, in all the sheds.
Everybody brought unwanted cats to me.
When I walked to the mailbox,
cats followed me there
and followed me back to the house.
Some children thought I was a witch,
and neighbors complained about the smell.
If anybody asked me how many cats I had,
I'd always say ten.
It seemed like a reasonable number.

I hope somebody took care of the cats
after I was gone.
When first I was buried,
I thought occasionally
I could feel a cat's paws on my grave,
but after I was moved,
no cat could ever find me.

Joseph Strong Patterson
1889-1953

Joseph Strong Patterson

1889-1953

When I was a boy in Enfield,
I did chores for Mr. and Mrs. Potter.
One time she gave me lemonade,
but he was kinder still.
I guess he knew my father died that spring.
Mr. Potter was a famous sculptor.
I was proud he showed me the sketches
of the horses he made for statues of General Grant
and General Hooker. Some other artist made the
    men's figures.
He talked about the work with me
as if I was a real person.
When I grew up, I took my children to see
the statues in Boston and Philadelphia
and I told them all about Mr. Potter.,
We even saw the lions he made
for the New York Public Library.
They all made me feel
as if I were a part of forever.

Elvira Kimball Hill

1782-1849

Elvira Kimball Hill

1782-1849

I was born in Prescott.
How my mother hated the place.
She called it primitive
and insisted that I had to be a lady.
My father taught me how to read,
but my mother taught me needlecraft,
and I started a sampler
using lines from *Proverbs*.
They are my favorites, and Mother approved.
"Her ways are ways of pleasantness, and all her
　　paths are peace."
Mother thought the words would serve me well
because I was high spirited.
Sadly, Mother died when I was ten,
and I had to take care of Father.
I helped him with his sermons.
My sisters went to live with cousins.
I grew too busy for time with needlework,
and I put away my sampler.
Father remarried. He was called to a church in
　　Connecticut,
and my sisters joined him there.
I married Joshua Hill, the next minister of Prescott.

Ellen Page Barstow
1840-1915

Ellen Page Barstow

1840-1915

Charley and I had a farm in Prescott.
We had dairy cows and chickens
so we could sell milk, cheese, and eggs to the store.
We kept the animals in the barn
along with a fine pair of work horses.
Everything went along smoothly.
In the fall, we'd butcher a couple of pigs,
and we never went without.
But one night close to the new century,
lightning struck the barn, starting a fire in the hay.
The flames seemed joyful as they climbed the walls,
but their joy was our sorrow.
Charley burned his hands
trying to get to the horses.
He was never the same man after.
The fire destroyed the barn and all the animals.
Their screams haunted me till the day I died.

Jan Roos

1889-1950

Jan Roos

1889-1950

I came through Ellis Island
where I was met by a cousin
who lived in Springfield, Massachusetts.
I stayed with him and his wife
until I got lonesome for country air.
I found work at the box factory in North Dana,
    Massachusetts.
When the dam was to be built,
the factory sold out.
My cousin was dead by then,
and I knew nobody else from my country.
Anyway, I had to go where work was,
and I lived out my days in a rooming house in
    Athol.

Alice Byrnes Tedley
1901-1976

Alice Byrnes Tedley

1901-1976

Is there anybody left to remember
the last days of Enfield?
I danced the last dance
with my husband, Harold Tedley.
He wasn't much of a dancer,
but we really didn't feel much like dancing.
When the bells pealed for midnight
and we knew the town had died,
Harold's sweet tenor soared
above the others who were singing
"Auld Lang Syne."
We moved to Springfield
but reserved space in the new cemetery.
Harold rests beside me now.

Alice Brody
1882-1936

Alice Brody

1882-1936

There was no counting the number of beds
I made at the Quabbin Inn every summer.
Folks came for the fresh air
and good country food.
Most of the guests were nice people
and appreciated what we did for them,
but once in a while,
a spoiled prince or princess
complained about the food and the service.
There was no pleasing them.
I wouldn't have traded my life for theirs,
for they found no joy in living.
It might have done them good to have
made a bed or two.

John C. Brace
1907-1931

John C. Brace

1907-1931

I was late driving home.
I had so much on my mind.
In three days I was getting married,
and who wouldn't worry,
getting married in the midst of the Depression?
Anyway, there was an icy patch.
I saw the deer in the road, touched the brakes,
and skidded into a tree.
In the morning, when they found me,
the ice was gone.
Of course, there was no deer.
They said I must have fallen asleep at the wheel.
It could be true.
Maybe I only dreamed the ice and the deer.

Asa Boyden

1884-1950

Asa Boyden

1884-1950

I worked in Greenwich
at the Jewish boys camp in summer.
They came out from the city,
Boston, New York, and Springfield.
Although I was uneasy at first,
I soon learned they are just boys.
They followed me about
asking about this flower or that rock.
They wondered, too, what I did all winter.
I told them about cutting ice on the pond.
Horses would plow the snow from the pond,
and we'd cut a channel in the ice
so we could push the squares to the
  icehouse on the shore.
We'd store it covered in sawdust.
In the summer, the icemen would deliver
as much as was wanted
to the iceboxes in the city.
By then, I'd be opening up the camp again,
getting it ready for the Jewish boys.
I wonder how many of them
fought in the war
and how many gold stars hung
in the windows of the houses
where men delivered our ice.

Lorenzo Marston
1774-1836

Lorenzo Marston

1774-1836

When I became postmaster in Greenwich
in the summer of 1826, I'd sound a bell
when the postrider arrived with the mail.
Townsfolk would gather in hopes
of hearing from loved ones far away.
Abner Flume's boy was a missionary to the Indians
and would write as often as he could.
I, for one, could not understand why he had to go away.
I know of several individuals in this town who could
use some missionary work. Abner'd often read
his letters in church and maybe the sinners
got to hear the Word anyway. Mostly the mail
was less interesting. Mattie Reynolds got news
from her sister in Salem. The postrider
   would bring newspapers
so we kept up with the political efforts of General Jackson,
although nobody I know would vote for him.
Also I was sure his wife would bring scandal to the man,
and that might not always serve us well.
I never read a newspaper or even a letter
that could plow my field
or put a penny in my pocket.
Still, we are all a part of the world.
We should be aware.
How else can we protect ourselves?

Martha Rogan Bernard
1845-1901

Martha Rogan Bernard

1845-1901

Sam Bernard and I never got along.
When I used to ponder
why we ever got married,
I'd look around and realize
the pickings were poor for both of us.
After our son was born,
we both agreed enough was enough.
I moved to one side of the house
and Sam to the other.
One night I woke up to hammering.
Sam was putting up a wall
dividing the house.
Some people might have called it a spite wall,
but it was more an agreement wall.
I no longer cooked for Sam,
and he'd no longer do my chores,
split wood for the stove,
or shovel the walk for me to get to the store.
I could charge things at the store,
and Sam would never argue about the bill.
I took care of the girls and the boy,
but when Sam, Junior finished his schooling,
he moved to his father's side.
He'd visit us sometimes,
but none of the children ever asked us
about the wall and why we stayed married like that.

Michael Anthony Noonan
1876-1961

Michael Anthony Noonan

1876-1961

They called me the Centennial baby.
It was just one hundred years
after the new country became our new country.
My father said there wasn't enough
to eat in the old country,
so he brought my mother here.
I was born cheerful,
but I learned early
to avoid my father's fists
when the drink was on him.
Other times, he was a good jokester,
and people liked him.
Every July 6, we'd go as a family to Springfield.
We'd take the Rabbit Run.
I was sorry there were no rabbits,
for I carried a slingshot,
but it was exciting to take a train
even though it stopped and started in short hops.
We were going to celebrate my Aunt Agnes's birthday.
We'd get off the train and walk up Liberty Street.
All the way to Hungry Hill from doorways and windows
people would call out, "Hey, Jimmy,"
to my father. I'd ask, "Who's that?"

and he'd say he didn't know.
Once my mother whispered to me,
"More people know Tom the Fool
than Tom the Fool knows."
I figured it out when I grew older
after the old man died.

Eleanor Clarke Bird
1817-1871

Eleanor Clarke Bird

1817-1871

The weather that year was most peculiar.
Thaws and freezes when least expected,
and by summer, stars seemed to be flying through
    the sky.
People were frightened.
Prophet William Miller preached that the end
    was near.
He had charts to prove the world would
come to an end on October 22,1843.
Of course, he had said another date earlier,
but this time he was sure.
We were to dress in our white ascension robes
and go up the highest hill we could find
to meet our Maker that night,
and we would hear the final trumpets of glory.
Many of us went. I accompanied my sister.
Some of the believers had even given away
all their possessions. I had not.
Finally, when the midnight hour passed,
there were no trumpets. By dawn
everybody felt a great disappointment.
We had to walk down the hill
in front of all the unbelievers,
many of whom were laughing.
I still had my home,
so my sister and I went there and stayed.
It was a long time before I ventured forth again.

Sophronia Foster
1802-1865

Sophronia Foster

1802-1865

I wrote all the verses
for neighbors in their grief
to cut upon gravestones
of people they loved.
Of course I did not expect payment, but I often received
    little gifts:
vegetables from their gardens, wood for my stove,
or a few eggs so I can make my sponge cake.
The churchyards in Enfield
are filled with my words,
but I saved my favorite
expecting it to be cut
when my time came.
She was always gentle.
She was always kind.
At home with the angels
she left earth behind.
But nobody saw to it.
They were too busy with the war,
and my stone is still unversed.

Matthew E. Harper
1846-1927

Matthew E. Harper

1846-1927

My brothers went out to Illinois
where they were giving out land,
acres and acres of good fertile land,
but I stayed home with my parents
who said they needed at least one of us to stay.
We had already cleared our land of stones
and laid foundations for houses and barns
with good solid fieldstone.
We raised sheep on the farm
and managed our lives well.
Nobody ever went hungry.
Even in the lean years, there was always enough.
When the people in Boston
started talking about taking our land,
I couldn't believe it.
We tried to fight, but they were too much for us.
I died in Greenwich, but they didn't let me stay there.
Could this have happened in Illinois?

Beatrice L. Granger
1832-1901

Beatrice L. Granger

1832-1901

My life was uneventful.
I was born to a nice family
who lived in a nice house.
When I was seventeen
I married a nice man.
We had two nice children
who lived and married nice people themselves.
But sometimes in church,
I'd want to stand up in the pew and shout,
"Lord, isn't there something
we should be doing?"
But a nice woman wouldn't do that.

Myrick Johnson
1887-1935

Myrick Johnson

1887-1935

Where did Charley Smith go?
He lived next door to me
in Smith's Village
in the big old house with the porch.
Once he invited me in,
and I saw framed photographs
of his white mother and his black father
side by side on the parlor wall.
Charley caught me looking at them,
and he told me that his mother was born in that house
but his father came up from Virginia
shortly after the slave times.
I always liked Charley.
He was a good neighbor.
Years later, some people tried to say
no Negroes lived in the Valley,
so I'd say, "What about Charley Smith?"
I wonder where he went when they took his house.

Lula Clermont

1860-1932

Lula Clermont

1860-1932

Everybody loved my bread-and-butter pickles.
Every year they'd bring me the blue ribbon
at the Grange Fair.
My friend Alice Dunning
asked me for the recipe one year,
and I shared it with her.
The next year her pickles took the prize,
and she had been a friend!
From then on, any recipe shared
would be missing one ingredient:
salt, spice, shortening, or half the sugar—
however I felt that day.
Eventually nobody asked me
for a recipe.
Not even friends.
But I never made
bread-and-butter pickles again.

Harley Gruber
1848-1923

Harley Gruber

1848-1923

Don't expect me to say anything.
I ain't a forgiving man.
Bad enough they took the house
I built where my son Mason was living
with his family . . . wife and three children,
but they had to move Martha and me here.
I was resting peacefully in Enfield
where Bigelow, the undertaker,
laid me to rest next to Martha.
But the government went ahead
and hired strangers, men from Boston,
to move me here.
You think I didn't complain
when I first heard the talk
about the government taking over the Swift River?
But who listened to an old man?
Nobody, that's who.
The Boston people pretended
to listen to our concerns,
but they went ahead
and did what they wanted.
You call that democracy?
Well, I don't, and that's all I'll say.

Carrie Lee Betts

1802-1871

Carrie Lee Betts

1802-1871

Gardens delight me. Especially flower gardens.
While I can admire other people's endeavors,
I am particularly proud of my own.
The business of other people's gardens
disquiets me from time to time.
For example, if I see Mrs. Ramsey, the lawyer's wife,
has a flourishing lily of a striking color,
I have been known to add a clump of it to my lilies.
If she wonders how I found that color,
I say a cousin in Salem sent it to me.
At night I can collect seeds
from almost anybody's garden.
If the owner accosts me, I then admit
to admiring her flowers.
That's always a forgivable offense.
Nobody has more foxgloves than I,
and I defy anybody to compete with my columbine.

Does anybody tend the garden still,
or have the weeds won?

Meshak Genner
1792-1827

Meshak Genner

1792-1827

A wedding band changes a woman.
Before she has it, she is mild as a lamb
and coos like a little white dove.
When she has the ring on her finger,
the true woman emerges.
My wife fooled me until our firstborn arrived.
After William's birth, I noticed her face had grown sour,
and I felt the venom of her sharp tongue.
The litany of her complaints grew month by month.
The cow broke the fence and trampled her garden.
Mice were nibbling at the flour bin.
The baby had colic, and William the earache.
The barn roof leaked, spoiling the hay.
There was never enough wood for the cookfire,
and there was hardly enough to cook.
Little wonder I preferred the company of my friends.
We'd light our pipes and share a bowl or two of
    punch
or whatever was going around that night.
They'd tell me what a fine fellow I was,
and we'd talk and dream of finding fortune.
Perhaps we'd go to the West or out to sea,
someplace to escape the eternal complaints of women.

Well, she's free of me now.
On winter's coldest night, walking home in darkness,
I slipped on ice and fell into the brook.
It was scarcely more than a trickle being
    clogged with ice.
There I took the chill which killed me.

Rufus Genner

1790-1861

Rufus Genner

1790-1861

I was ashamed of my brother,
dying the way he did and forcing me
to arrange his burial and buy a stone for him.
I felt for his wife too because she was left penniless.
A complaining wife she had been,
but she was once a pretty little thing,
and he led her a merry dance.
After the funeral and the few mourners had gone,
I told her I would look after her and the children.
I repaired what my brother had done,
and I did what he had not done
until the farm was trim and neat once again.
I noticed she smiled more,
and the children greeted me happily.
They'd search in my pockets for gingerbread,
and she'd ask me for advice on domestic matters.
I spent so much time with her,
it seemed only right to marry.
We had a good life together.
I raised my brother's children and my own equally.
Her manner to me was mild as a lamb,
and she always spoke sweetly.

Cornelia Watkins
1849-1902

Cornelia Watkins

1849-1902

For a long time I lived alone.
It was not that I had no suitors,
for I owned a good farm,
but their rough ways did not please me.
Then my cousin Julia Norris came to share my home.
For such a little thing, scarcely five feet tall,
she was very strong and could do almost anything.
She built the passageway from house to barn
which helped in winter storms when the cows needed
  milking.
She and our neighbor Abner Fuller slaughtered the pigs.
When it was done and the meat shared out,
she sat quietly all alone in the dark parlor for more than an
  hour.
I could kill chickens without a fuss, but they don't squeal,
and Julia was more sensitive than I.
I lost her the day she went out by herself to cut the trees
that were shading her hay fields.
She didn't come in to supper, so I went looking for her.
When I found her so still, so quiet, under a tree,
I ran to fetch Abner Fuller.
He hitched up his oxen and pulled the tree from her.
Abner picked up her broken body, cradled it in his arms,
and praised her for a good neighbor.
We laid her on the table in the parlor

to wait for the coffin to come.

Abner and his sons helped me in the seven yers I lived on.

In my will, I left my farm to Abner Fuller

for his great kindness to my Julia on that terrible day.

John M. Curtis
1897-1959

John M. Curtis

1897-1959

All I ever wanted was music.
When I was real little, they let me play triangle
with the town band. I kept time real good.
Eventually I graduated to a trombone,
and when I was thirteen, I sprouted up
so I could stretch my arms
to play those low notes.
We rehearsed on Thursdays in the school
so we'd be ready for any dance,
party, or parade on the weekend.
Mostly we played patriotic songs or dance music.
Once at a band concert,
we were playing, "Swing Low Sweet Chariot,"
and when we got to the low part,
I played the lowest notes I could.
Lo-o-o-o-w and stretched it out.
Mr. Duffy, the bandleader, didn't like it,
but the crowd loved it, especially Sally.
When I turned sixteen, I left school
and played in bands all over the country.
Some of them were almost famous, too.
Once I auditioned for Tommy Dorsey,

but he said he already had a trombone.
I'd come home whenever I could,
and when I was on the road, Sally wrote me
every single day all our married life.
I kept all the letters. There were lots of them.
I have them with me here.
We spent so much time apart
I'm grateful we're together now forever,
but sometimes I miss my trombone.

Minerva Pratt

1862-1930

Minerva Pratt

1862-1930

I sang in the church choir
for thirty-seven years.
Soprano. Every Sunday
and for weddings and funerals.
When Reverend McAllister called on me one day,
I thought he wanted to discuss hymns
for the next service,
but instead he intimated that
I was being selfish.
I should share the solos
with younger women
so they, too, could lift their voices to the Lord.
I can tell you I was stunned,
but I am a Christian so I forgave him.
I continued to pray in that church,
but I never sang again.
I put it in my will that I wanted no music at my funeral.

Elizabeth Ross

1860-1941

Elizabeth Ross

1860-1941

When I was a girl in Enfield,
we celebrated the Fourth of July properly.
We'd have a parade, a band concert, fireworks,
and the Civil War veterans marched in uniform
wearing their medals and carrying flags.
There was an even bigger celebration
for the Centennial in 1876.
Everybody had fireworks.
Stevie Potter lost three fingers on his right hand,
but we said it was in a good cause.
When I had to move and found myself in
    West Brookfield,
I found celebrations didn't exist.
My disappointment was overwhelming.
The next Fourth of July, I got myself a drum
and pinned a red, white, and blue ribbon on my hat,
and I marched around the common by myself
banging on my drum for an hour.
By Heaven, wherever I am on the Fourth of July,
there'll be a celebration for America.
Maybe it's my name, Betsy Ross,
but I've always been a patriot.

Joseph Strong, Jr.
1917-1942

Joseph Strong, Jr.

1917-1942

I looked like an athlete,
a farm boy with a strong back,
so they wanted me to play every game . . . at first.
My father loved baseball,
and I wanted him to be proud of me
so I tried out for baseball in high school.
It was a small school without much competition.
I made the team, and they put me in center field.
How I prayed that no one would hit a fly ball to me.
I could bat respectably, so they kept me on the team.
I liked the feeling of swinging the bat out,
hitting the ball as hard as I could.
When all the talk came
about Boston taking our river,
I breathed a sigh of relief. I'd be free of this place.
I had visions of Paris and Art with a capital *A*.
But my father enrolled me in Stockbridge,
the school of agriculture in Amherst.
They had a baseball team, too.
I graduated and went to work for my father.
With the Depression on, there were no other jobs.
Right after Pearl Harbor, I joined the navy
in hopes that I'd see the world . . . maybe even
     get to Paris.
My ship was attacked by a Japanese war plane,

and I was shot on deck by a stray bullet.
They sent my body here eventually.
My father put my name on every war memorial,
and he put a gold star in his window.
I finally made him proud.

Isabel Morton

1881-1945

Isabel Morton

1881-1945

We lived next door to the Harrelsons.
Their boys were limbs of Satan, and no wonder.
Nobody paid them any attention.
Their mother always had her head in a book
while the boys ran roughshod over the neighborhood.
I never said a word to anybody,
and when I'd make some little comment to Harry,
he'd always tell me, "Mind your business, Isabel."
I did until the day I looked out the window
and saw the boys with their little sister. She
   was only three
and followed them around like a puppy.
She had put her head on a wooden block
while one of the boys, Johnny I think, fetched a hatchet.
I ran out of my house screaming like a stuck pig.
The boys said they were playing French Revolution.
Well, I said a few choice words to their mother,
and she called me an interfering old biddy.
I was glad they moved before we did.
Let the town of Ware look after them, I say.
We moved to a bungalow in South Hadley,
and I never gave another thought to the Harrelsons.

Abigail R. Spellman
1802-1886

Abigail R. Spellman

1802-1886

I raged against my daughter-in-law.
I bore fourteen children,
seven of whom lived.
The others died before anyone else knew them.
They are all here someplace,
as is my daughter-in-law.
Whenever visitors came for me,
or even if Edmund asked me a question,
she would speak for me—
"She likes this. She says that."
Until I was ready to scream in rage.
Finally I grew silent.
There was no purpose in my trying to speak.

Joanna L. Spellman
1836-1900

Joanna L. Spellman

1836-1900

Edmund's mother lived with us
the last years of her life.
I did everything for that woman—
washed her clothes, cooked her food,
made her bed. Did she appreciate it?
I think not. She would strike out in rage
and hit me. Not that I ever told Edmund.
I guess she resented me because I was young,
and she was very old. She raged,
and she took it out on me.
I did my Christian duty,
but I didn't shed a tear at her funeral.

Levi Garston

1797-1893

Levi Garston

1797-1893

I lived a fine life
working the land in Prescott.
My farm was small,
but I grew enough food
to feed my family.
My fingers loved to feel soil.
I'd plant carefully,
pushing my fingers into the dirt
to make a place for the seed.
The harvest was satisfying,
but I loved best the planting.
One hot summer day, I fell asleep in the garden,
and I didn't wake up.
My only regret is that the women who prepared me
   for burial
washed my hands and cleaned
the dirt from under my fingernails.
Such little things are meaningful for eternity.

Bruce Denholm
1864-1936

Bruce Denholm

1864-1936

I kept a small store
which answered my needs,
but my passion was fishing.
I graduated from a pole and string
when I was a boy
to a rod and reel in a boat for trolling.
The spinners flashed behind in the water
as we slowly paddled around the lake.
Finally I discovered fly fishing.
What a joy that was.
I stood alone close to shore.
All was quiet as I cast.
My reel hummed as the line fed out.
Suddenly a trout grabbed the fly.
I played the line
slowly, carefully until the fish tired
and I could bring it into my net.
Too small, I would unhook it and toss it back.
Eventually I kept no fish
but I continued the sport.
I tied a new fly
and named it the Green Witch.
It brought me many a trout.

E. P.

1815-1828

E. P.

1815-1828

My name is Enoch Parker.
I was born in Enfield. That's all I knew.
I cursed the overseers of the poor
every day of my life because
they hounded my poor mother
until she died of shame and want.
They wanted her to name my father,
but she never did.
I was six years old and could print my name.
Lawyer Gedney said he had need of a boy
to live in his barn and care for his cows.
I would lead them out to pasture
in the morning and back again at night.
Wintertimes they kept me warm.
I was small for my age
and my hands too small for milking,
but I earned my small keep.
The task I feared most was drowning the kittens.
Twice a year, the barn cats would hide their litters,
and I had to find them.
Once I found a nice rock, and I decided to
  carve my name.
I wanted something of my own.
I chipped out the first letters,

but the rock was hard and I had no real tools.
One day I stepped on a rusty nail
and got sick soon after.
I think I was put in a pauper's grave,
but maybe some kindly soul set my rock
upon my grave so eternity could find me.

William D. Heinrich
1904-1962

William D. Heinrich

1904-1962

Machines spoke my language,
and I spoke theirs.
I used to take everything apart
to put back together, so
when my father bought a used John Deere,
he had seen left out in a field to rust
after the owner died, I was in my glory.
It was a 1920 model with the green paint
all chipped and rusted.
I could tinker and putter all day long.
I got her painted and polished up
and I kept that tractor purring like
a well-fed kitten.
Folks around would call on me
to fix whatever motor wasn't working right,
even Fords and one old LaSalle.
I could do it, and I made a little money.
I had no use for schooling or for farming,
but I had to honor my father, so I farmed.
When my father moved the family to a
farm in Hadley,
he helped me buy my own house,
and I then got a family of my own.
When Father left off farming,

I got a regular job at Roe's garage in Amherst.
I could spend my days covered in grease.
I was a happy man.
Of course, I kept the old tractor in good shape.
When the garage closed, I turned back
to small engine repair. We got by on that.
When my father died, I inherited the old tractor.
Like me, it was useful for small jobs.

Abigail Parsons
1901-1974

Abigail Parsons

Beloved Wife of John Parsons

1901-1974

We met in Enfield, married there,
and started our family. Two boys and a girl.
John worked the family farm with his brother.
The boys helped as they grew up,
but none of the children took to farming.
John, Junior went to college and became a teacher.
Bill joined the Navy. I was sorry,
because I hoped to keep the boys nearby.
Ellen married and lives in Connecticut.
When we had to leave the farm,
John and his brother each bought a place
in Granby, Massachusetts and divided up the animals.
Both of them shared the farm machines. No sense
in buying more than what was needed.
Sharing is good.
After the children started their own lives,
John and I grew close again. We were
 good companions.
I took to helping him with the cows.
Mornings we would go to the barn
where the cows would be waiting.
In winter, you could see your breath in the air,
but for summer, windows were open.
We'd have fresh air, and we could watch the sun rise.
The sound of the milk in the pails

was comforting. Swoosh-swoosh. I missed it
when we got milking machines.
I could still help, though.
I'd wash and disinfect the pails and machine parts
while John cleaned out the stalls.
Then I'd see to breakfast.
John would wash his hands and face.
We'd sit at the table companionably
and share stories from the newspaper
while we ate our breakfast.
I suppose I'm being sentimental,
but it seems to me a shared life is a lovely one.

Rachel Newton
1827-1863

Rachel Newton

1827-1863

When my dear sister Annie went out west
with her husband, I wept for days
until Jeremiah reminded me to accept God's will.
It was always hard for me to be obedient,
as I had always been a self-willed child.
Our first born was a girl,
and Jeremiah suggested we call her Annie.
I loved him for that, but then I realized
he had no interest in the child.
She was only a girl.
He was happier when the twins came.
Two boys, Joshua and Josephus.
Annie was a year old by then and had learned
not to hold out her little arms to her father.
Then we had Jemima and Lemuel.
Jeremiah was pleased there were boys enough
to work the farm. I could teach the girls
housekeeping, sewing, and cooking.
Then little Annie caught a fever and died,
and I thought my heart would break.
I washed her and put her in her christening dress.
She seemed so tiny in the box Jeremiah fashioned.
I knew there was a photographer staying at the
    hotel in town,
and I begged Jeremiah to let me have a remembrance.
He gave in. The twins picked wild flowers,

and the photographer came all the way up the hill
to take Annie's picture surrounded by flowers.
I asked him to make two pictures so
I could send one to my sister.
It was important for her to see her namesake
even in death.
How else could she know her in the hereafter?

George Winship
1914-1987

George Winship

1914-1987

My dog Gypsy went everywhere with me.
I had her since she was a tiny pup scarcely weaned.
She was the best of dogs, a shepherd mix,
the kind of dog you'd always see in a farmyard.
At first I didn't understand
why she'd bump into things,
but then I saw that she was totally blind.
My father told me to get rid of her,
but she was smart and so eager to please.
We understood each other.
I'd whistle if we were walking along
and there was something in her way
so she'd walk around it. That's how smart she was.
If I'd forget and she bumped into a stone or something,
she'd give me a sorrowful look, and I'd feel bad.
Gypsy followed me to school, and she'd wait outside.
If I was kept after school, she'd come find me,
and the teacher would say, "Gypsy's here. Go on home,"
but I shouldn't do whatever I did ever again.
She'd even follow me to church.
She wanted to go in, but my mother'd give me a look,
and I'd say, "Wait, Gypsy" so she'd wait outside.
Sometimes I'd hear her sing with the soprano, and
the people would be laughing.
Reverend Pollard didn't like that

and told me to keep her at home.
It was easier then not to go to church.
Reverend Pollard didn't like that either.
Neither did my mother, so she talked to him
    about Gypsy,
and he invited me to come back to church.
We could sit in the back row, and I'd keep her
    quiet for the singing.
She lived to a good age, sixteen,
but she slowed down considerably her last years.
I'd have to walk slow so she could keep up.
She still slept by my bed and one morning
    didn't wake.
I buried her on the farm near the garden.
When they came to move all the graves,
they left Gypsy behind. She's there under the water,
and I am way over here.
I still think there's something not right about that.

Theodocia Parrish

1881-1936

Theodocia Parrish

1881-1936

I graduated from New Salem Academy
and went on to Fitchburg for further education.
Then I taught for many years in Greenwich
until I was forced to leave.
I think the leaving killed me.
For most of my life, the talk
was all about the state taking the town.
People fought it. Elected officials went so far
as to say we fought the Huns to protect our homes—
what had our brave boys fought and died for?
We hoped our wishes would prevail.
It was not to be.

I remember the celebration for the Fourth of July in 1922.
The Monson Band played,
and there was a parade with floats and flags.
I was asked to run in the fat women's race,
but I declined. Hattie Walker won with a
    woman from Barre
whose name I don't recollect.
Greenwich won the baseball game with Enfield.
Altogether it should have been a happy day,
but the speeches were all about leaving.

The leaving took many, many years.

I watched families scatter,
orchards cut down,
houses broken and taken away.
I saw my schoolhouse dismantled,
broken up, and what could not be sold
was burned to the ground.
It will never be a schoolhouse again.
Greenwich was bereft of all we valued.
It would have been easier
if it had happened quickly like a real flood.
As it was, it was like dying a little bit at a time.

Rufus Willard
1917-1976

Rufus Willard

1917-1976

Our last day in Enfield was busy.
First the cows had to be loaded onto the truck.
They were nervous, but my dog Alfie nipped their heels
so they rushed onto the truck to get away from him.
Then Alfie and I had to bring in the heifers
from out of the far pasture.
The hill was steep, but I didn't dare run
because the grass was still wet from the dew.
Alfie was the hero,
hurrying the young cows along.
Another truck was waiting in the yard
by the time we got there.
The heifers were confused and afraid.
They knew that truck had come before
to take away the old cows and the bull calves.
They tried not to go, but Alfie herded them on.
I looked around the yard once more.
It looked sad and empty,
but we couldn't stay there any more.
I joined the driver and the dog in the front seat.
Alfie rode with his head out the window.
His mouth was open as if he was laughing.
My head was full of questions, and I was quiet.
I went back years later, and I stood on that hill

where the heifers had been pastured and
    looked at the water.
My life saw many changes, some good, some bad,
but it seems to me that one was the hardest.

Miriam Alvirah Price
1844-1911

Miriam Alvirah Price

1844-1911

I cannot deny that Henry was different.
Even as a baby, he looked different.
He was born shortly after my husband died.
We'd had a store in Dana,
and I kept it after I was widowed.
My older son Michael wanted nothing to do
with the store, with Dana, and especially with Henry.
He had been devoted to his father,
and somehow, in his mind, the wrong parent lived.
Henry grew strong and healthy,
but you could tell his mind was slow.
I sent him to school, of course, but one January day
he ran home. His chin was bloody and his coat sleeve.
When he could finally get the words out,
he told me a big boy told him to touch his tongue to the
    school fence,
said it would taste like honey.
He said all the boys laughed.
Henry never told me which boy it was,
but I elected to take him out of school.
I could teach him everything he needed—
his name and address, how to tie his shoes,
    useful things.
We spent days playing store together

and learning to make change.
Henry was growing to be a man, and I worried.
Frustration would bring on a fit of temper,
out of control, slamming doors, throwing whatever was in his hand
against the wall, breaking glass.
I had to be careful that nobody ever saw that.
Nonetheless, people were afraid of Henry. He was
   very strong.
It got so very few customers came to the store.
I didn't know how we could continue.
Then I discovered I was sick, and
I wouldn't get better.
What would become of Henry then?
I had found mushrooms in the morning,
and I cooked them in butter and
left some on the stove.
Let them think what they will.
Then Henry came in with flowers.
He had picked them by pulling,
and the roots hung below the bouquet.
I said, "Henry, let's have our tea now."
I cut the bread and butter into little pie shapes
the way he specially loved, and I poured the tea.
I urged him to have all the honey he wanted.
He stirred and stirred his cup
before he drank it, and I let him put honey in mine.

When his was all gone, I drank mine.
I held his hand when his cramps started,
as long as I could until I could feel my cramps begin.
God knows I did it out of love.

Henry Price
1885-1911

Henry Price

1885-1911

I can tie my shoes myself,
and I know all the coins by name.
I'm a big boy, and I take care of Mother.
I can carry her anywhere she wants to go.
My brother Michael can't do that.
He never even comes to see us.
After he left home, it was just Mother and me.
Every afternoon, we have tea together.
I like mine with honey. Lots of honey.

Cassie Birdsell

1821-1876

Cassie Birdsell

1821-1876

We made a signature quilt
for Julia Stacy who had told us
that she and Alden were moving out west
to the Nebraska Territory.
"Aren't you afraid of the Indians?"
Lena Massey asked, but Julia said that was settled.
White families were safe now.
She said Alden Stacy was weary
of fighting the stones in Prescott.
"Let the rocks take over," he said. "The new land
is open and easy to plow. Good soil, too."
When I told that to Hosea Birdsell,
he said that Alden Stacy was always a flighty man.
He'd rather find something new
than finish up a job already started.
Hosie said that he, for one,
would not put his family to risk like that.
Better to stay safe at home.
Of course, I couldn't say any of that to Julia.
Instead, all the ladies of the church
wrote their names in ink on white squares in the quilt.
We gave it to Julia as a parting gift
with our love and many tears.

Ralph C. Manning
1907-1986

Ralph C. Manning

1907-1986

My family put off leaving
as long as we could.
After a while, as the houses emptied
and the fields gave themselves back to the woods,
it got too hard to stay. I left with the family,
but Greenwich was the only home I'd ever known.
Later I'd go back with the others sometimes.
We'd meet at the administration building by the dam.
By then I'd retired and had the time.
I'd look at the water,
and in my imagination it was all still there
just as it had been. Walker's Sawmill,
the post office, Sloan's Store, and the Quabbin Inn.
The spire of the Congregational church still housed
the bell to call us to Sunday services.
Of course in my heart I knew it wasn't real.
The last time I went back, my daughter drove me.
It was 1982 or '83. I can't remember which.
Anyway, it had been dry that year, and the
　　water was low.
Your eyes could still follow the road
that led down into the water.

Only the road was cracked and broken,
and you could see the remains of stone walls.
I accepted the fact that there was nothing left.
Nothing to mark the place where I had lived.

Rebecca Peters
1801-1876

Rebecca Peters

1801-1876

Mother was scarcely cold
when Clarissa started making decisions.
First she took the cameo from Mother's dresser.
Father had bought it for Mother when he went to
   the State House.
It was the profile of a Roman goddess.
She said," This should come to me as the oldest girl."
We were all assembled in the parlor,
Clarissa and Jonas, Benjamin with Lavinia,
   Graham and Mary,
and me with my dear Noble.
She then said, looking at Benjamin, "Of course,
this house will be sold and the proceeds divided."
Benjamin suggested that haste was unseemly.
There would have been a quarrel
but for the arrival of Reverend Hawes and his wife.
They had come to pray with us.
Later Graham said he thought Mother had
   made a will.
Graham had studied law for a year before he
   went into banking.
Clarissa was sure that Father's will arranged the estate,
but Graham assured us that Father
left the house and one hundred acres to Mother outright.
I had never lived in any other home.

Noble and I married and our children were born there.
I was glad that Graham was proved right,
but Clarissa was outraged because Mother
willed the house, contents, and land to Noble and me.
I had taken care of the house all my life,
and we took loving care of Mother after Father's death.
I did not want to appear to be selfish, though.
I gave the family portraits to Benjamin
since he carried our father's name.
Graham was pleased to have the Governor Winthrop desk
and the painting on glass of General Washington.
Then I meted out Mother's earrings and brooches
to Lavinia and Mary. They were welcome to some of
    the quilts, too.
Clarissa and Jonas left Enfield right after the funeral.
She never mentioned Mother's cameo,
and I never asked for it back,
but after she had gone,
I discovered it carelessly pinned to Mother's pillow.
Mother would have regretted
dissension in the family,
but Clarissa never forgave me.

Laurinda Perkins

1837-1901

Laurinda Perkins

1837-1901

I suffered from headaches
and what Mother would have called the vapors
since my husband died. Junius
was a responsible man and left me
provided for decently. But my house was lonely.
so I invited my son Amos to come home
with his family. I had no idea
how loud his boys were, and their mother
had no idea how to control them.
The girls were bad enough chattering,
but, oh, the boys! My headaches grew even worse.
Dr. Sweetser, the family doctor, could do nothing for me.
Then Abby Prater who worked in my kitchen
    suggested
that I try Hostetter's Bitters. It helped her.
Well, I got some at the store,
and right off I started feeling good,
more like my old self again.
I wouldn't hesitate to recommend it
to all my friends. Amos is afraid
there is an alcohol content, but I say
it's my medicine and it's doing me good.
I keep it with me all day long.
We've always been Temperance in this family,
and I, for one, would never touch spirits,

but I'm keeping my medicine
whatever Amos says. Any morning
I have a headache, I reach for my medicine.
It's like a miracle cure.

Gordon Blackstone

1801-1872

Gordon Blackstone

1801-1872

I never was a lawyer.
Don't hold with the breed.
They'd say they'd represent you,
but you'd find yourself represented to the poor farm.
My father taught me that.
He went to law over the neighbor's
use of our pastureland.
We ended up with no pasture at all
because their lawyer proved we had no clear title.

No goin' to law for me. No sir.
I'd rather keep what I have.
I can look out of my window
and see my field and my sheep,
my pigs and the beef cow.
I know what's what, and no lawyer's
goin' to fool me into payin'
him for cheatin' me.

Joseph Curland
1810-1872

Joseph Curland

1810-1872

What a joke are we human beings.
We think we own the world
because we walk upright and use words,
and our thumbs and fingers allow us
to work machines, write with pens,
comb hair, sew, knit, and shoot guns.
We are the lords of all we survey,
and what do we do?
We stand at machines or follow behind them all day
in exchange for scraps of paper or stamped metal disks
which we use to acquire what we need
and what we don't need.
Even a monkey is cleverer than that.
Those few who think
think for us, and we follow their wishes
more like sheep than our closer relatives.
If there is a god, I hope he's pleased
with his creations. I am not.
Not even my own children please me.
They follow their mother to church
like goslings to a pond with the goose.
I must say that I despise my wife's simplicity.
She claims the books I read will cast me to the flames.
She even glorifies the son who was killed in the war.
To her he was a hero, martyred

for the Union and the Brotherhood of Man.
How many more sons will she sacrifice
before she learns that brotherhood is all illusion?
Even the book she reads so religiously
tells of Adam's sons, and one murders the other.

Carrie Shelton
1840-1910

Carrie Shelton

1840-1910

From his horse cart, Seneca Bartlett would leave me
sheaves of palm straw to make into hats.
I'd split the straw into fine strands,
and then I'd braid the strands into a pattern.
By working at home, I could take care of things,
keep the fire, and watch the children.
Dinner would be on the table when Charley
    came in at noon.
Then I'd get the dishes washed
and the children down for their naps.
If all was quiet, I'd work on the sheaves,
soak them until they were pliable,
and then, I'd take the braided circle
and shape a hat onto the forms I had.
One for the Panamas, one for the Shaker bonnets.
If it stayed quiet, I could get several done.
Splitting and weaving the strips of palm
was hard on the hands. The edges were sharp.
At first, it was very difficult,
but gradually I got used to it.
When Mr. Bartlett returned, he'd pile the hats onto
    his cart,
give me more sheaves to work on. I'd pay for the
    sheaves,

and he'd pay for the hats or bonnets he was taking to
the Dana factory.

I never had idle hands
for the devil to put to use.
Charley was proud of me
for earning a little extra.
We put the money away for a rainy day.

Harry Seymour Smith
1871-1939

Harry Seymour Smith

1871-1939

Eugene never liked houses.
He was outdoors all seasons.
"Camping out" he called it.
Sometimes when the ice and snow were bad,
he'd let himself into somebody's summer cottage
and light up the wood stove. Somehow,
he always knew where there'd be dry wood enough
and who left behind a blanket or two.
He had no job, not a regular one anyway,
but somehow he scraped by.
Often he'd let us boys tag along,
and as we grew older, he taught us about the woods.
He could track a deer soundlessly
like an Indian, but he never hunted
except for food for himself or his old parents.
After they died, he stayed pretty much by himself,
and we scarcely gave him another thought
until one winter's day we passed by a summer cottage
on Lake Neeseponsett. An open door seemed like an
  invitation
but from the steps we could see Eugene
sitting as if asleep on a rocking chair.
Of course, one of us went to tell the authorities.
Eugene would be buried at the town's expense.
Enfield had already taken his parents' house

because no taxes had been paid for years.
We let them take Eugene to town.
He was placed in a closed pine box,
and we worried because Eugene would have
    despised that.
That night, four of us got to the church,
opened the box, and rescued Eugene.
We put in boards to make up for his weight
and hammered the lid closed.
We rowed Eugene out to the middle of the lake
which hadn't frozen over yet. We had tied
stones to his body, lifted him out of the boat,
and let him sink slowly to the bottom.
No one was ever the wiser.
But I wondered what people thought when they dug up
his empy coffin.
Couldn't have worried much because
his stone is here as if Eugene himself was.

George S. Philbrick
1861-1905

George S. Philbrick

1861-1905

When I was fourteen,
we boarded one of the two Chinese boys
who were sent to Enfield to school by the Chinese
   government.
Mother was nervous for fear that they
   wouldn't be Christian,
but when she discovered they were,
she was quite proud of the work
she had done for the missionary society.
I had to share my room with Chung Lee
and I wasn't too pleased about it.
The other boy boarded with Mr. and Mrs. Harvey.
He had his own room there,
but Chung Lee never said that boy was better off.
He was nice enough, I guess,
but it was hard on me because Father expected me
to keep up with him in school. I tried,
but Chung Lee was very smart in all subjects,
especially in math. I was better in English class,
but then, of course, I had an advantage.
I doubt I could have done as well as he in Chinese.
We both graduated, and both of us went on to
   Amherst College.
By then, I wasn't worrying about trying to keep up
   with him.

He was going to study for the ministry.
It might have pleased my mother,
but I went into the law. I practiced in Enfield my
   whole life,
and Chung Lee went back to China.
He died of a fever there when he was twenty-five.
It's a good thing for me I had stopped trying to
   keep up with him.

Thankful Perkins
1756-1846

Thankful Perkins

Wife and Mother

1756-1846

Nahum built a small house when we first married.
He said it would be easier to add
than to build more than we needed at first.
But then we had no need to build on
because we were not blessed with issue.
I tried not to envy others in church
surrounded by their children.
Then I saw their suffering when a child dies.
Fever took little Rebecca Carter and Asa Biddle.
I was thankful, indeed, that no child of mine
would suffer in that way.
God's will be done.
When Salome Biddle caught the fever,
I nursed her. On her deathbed, I promised
that I would care for her little ones
as if they were my own.
Their father died at Yorktown.
Nahum built the children's wing, adding to our house.
He and I sat in our pew on Sundays
surrounded by the Biddle children.
Let us praise God. His will be done.

Ransom Hathaway, Esq.
1812-1865

Ransom Hathaway, Esq.

1812-1865

My life was busy, industrious,
leaving no stone unturned
on my way to achieving money
and importance. I was admired and respected
as treasurer of the church and selectman.
I think my lawyering served my clients well,
and yet, when I knew I was dying,
my heart regretted all the things I didn't do.
I never told my father I loved him,
nor did I thank my wife. I simply assumed she would
    be there
any time I needed her. As for my sons?
Who taught them right from wrong?
Who guided them through thorny paths?
Not I. I was busy.
How trivial my importance now
when I think I could have shared
in my children's games and taught them
what I knew of the night sky.
Traveller, take heed as you pass by.

Charity Damon Bartlett
1812-1871

Charity Damon Bartlett

1812-1871

My Seneca would get up mornings
looking for his breakfast,
porridge and bacon cooked crisp,
eggs fried in the bacon grease,
a slice of bread. Every morning the same.
He'd go off for the day to fill his cart with palm leaves
for the ladies in town to make hats for the factory.
I often asked him why he wouldn't let me.
He said that he loved that my hands were soft.
"You are a lady," he'd say. I grant you
I came from a good family,
but I could have worked with the best of them
if Seneca permitted. Instead, he hired a girl
for heavy cleaning, and he brought in a pump
for the soapstone sink. I had water in my kitchen!
He was very good to me,
and I did my best to keep him happy.

Benjamin M. Toller

1817-1891

Benjamin M. Toller

1817-1891

I liked to touch wood.
The feel of a board I sanded and oiled
would fill me with satisfaction.
From a boy, I knew it would be my life's work.
I could build almost anything,
turn maple into drawer fronts dovetailed with
    birch or ash sides.
I made most of the desks for the Center School
in Enfield. When Lucas Potter asked me
to make his office desk, I found the perfect
    cherry boards.
I delighted in the glow of the wood—
the more I polished, the more it
    glowed under my hand.
I rarely got such a commission, though.
Most of my work was simple carpentry.
Anyone was welcome to come to my workshop.
I enjoyed the company. We'd sit by the stove
and talk about things important to us,
matters of life and death. It was common
for me to be called out after a death
to measure this one or that for a coffin.
I never admitted that I had most of the measurements
already in a little notebook I kept in my workshop.
I could measure a living man by walking next to him.

A dead man was no different.
Women were more difficult for me.
I could get the height, but I was afraid
they'd misunderstand if I looked too long.
For myself, I started to make a beautiful maple box,
but Wilson Smith admired the wood and asked me
to make a blanket chest as a gift for his wife.
I did that again and again.
When I died, young Reginald Baker
measured me and made me a simple pine box.
It will do for eternity, but he didn't finish sanding it.
There is a splinter by my right side.

Eleanor Clement
1899-1980

Eleanor Clement

1899-1980

I was born in Enfield
and lived there until I went to Worcester.
There I went to secretarial school
and landed a position with the school superintendent
on graduation. I met and married Carl Sorenson.
We had no children, so I kept on working.
I clipped all the newspaper accounts about
    the reservoir
and saved them for my parents in Enfield.
Naturally, I went home every weekend to help
them move from Enfield when it was time.
They were heartbroken, and I hoped they'd
    move near me.
We could buy a big house and share it,
but Dad couldn't move that far away.
They bought a place in Ware, and every day
Dad went back to watch the waters rise.
One Sunday night when I got back to the apartment,
Carl had had a drink or two.
I was disgusted and told him so.
Then he said he had met someone, someone else.
He wanted a divorce. I gave in when he said she
    was pregnant.
I took back my own name and went on.
Years later. I saw a graduation picture of his daughter.
I admit I teared up. She was a pretty girl.

By then I had friends, girls from the office
    and from the church.
We played bridge once a week, and I went on
    vacation with them.
We did have a good time together, but the
    group broke up.
Nancy died suddenly, and Alice remarried so
    she had no time for us.
Myra bought a place in Florida. I visited her once
but I didn't enjoy Florida at all. It didn't seem real.
After my stroke, I moved into the Sunset Home,
and I spent my last years in front of the TV
with new friends who didn't know me.
Sometimes, I'd forget they couldn't hear me,
and I'd speak up with a warning,
"Don't go there!" I'd say. "It's not safe."
But they'd go on as if I hadn't spoken.
When I was brought here to rest,
sharing a stone with my mother and father,
I thought I'd miss Worcester, but I didn't.
Instead I miss my new friends,
the ones who didn't know me,
and I wonder if Rachel got married again.

Daniel Parker Newman
1918-2005

Daniel Parker Newman

1918-2005

My father and mother moved from Dana
when the reservoir was still a rumor.
He said it was inevitable. Everything would go,
and he did not want to watch.
Secretly, my mother was happy to leave the farm.
She wanted to be part of what she called the
   real world.
Dad may have agreed because he took us to Amherst
when he got a job at Mass Aggie.
He never spoke of Dana, and we went back only once
when the Metropolitan District Commission
   notified him
that they were going to move graves.
His mother and father were laid to rest in Dana
but would be moved to the new cemetery
unless he had other plans for them. He hadn't.
Mother did not want to go so he took me with him
the day they were to be moved.
He said he had to be sure things were done right.
We first went to the Dana cemetery. He was quiet
and answered none of my questions about the farm.
There was a hearse at the cemetery already.
He and I stood by the graveside with
   Reverend Dawkins,
and when the digger's shovel hit on one coffin,

I saw a tear trickle down my father's cheek.
It was the only time he ever had showed any emotion.
We followed the hearse to the new
    Quabbin Park Cemetery
and stood by an open grave on a hill near
    some young pines
while Reverend Dawkins said a prayer.
They lowered the coffins respectfully
and mixed some dirt from the old cemetery
with dirt from the new as they filled the graves.
Dad thanked Reverend Dawkins and the diggers.
As we left the cemetery, he said,
"You have to see that things are done right."
When my mother died, she chose to be
    buried in Amherst,
but I was surprised to discover that
when my father's time came
he wanted to be laid to rest with his parents.
I saw to it and followed him there myself eventually.

Final Words

Now the final question is, of course,
what do they know
those many thousands gone?
Do they know the seasons?
Feel the snow in the graveyard
or shiver when the grass is cut?
Can they see the summer lightning
splitting the sky and then a tree nearby?
Do they wake some nights
to see the stars
or the moon's reflection on the water?
Are they aware of men and women fishing
in boats on the water above their towns?
Do they know of us visiting their graves
or have they left this all behind
and sleep and dream
of towns where houses still stand?

Text and captions for *A Swift River Anthology* are set in Palatino, a
large typeface family that began as an old style serif typeface
designed by Hermann Zapf
released in 1948 by the Linotype foundry.
In 1999, Zapf revised Palatino for Linotype and Microsoft, and
it was called Palatino Linotype.
The revised family incorporated extended
Latin, Greek, and Cyrillic character sets.
Titles were set in Kabel, a geometric sans-serif typeface
designed by German typeface designer Rudolf Koch and
released by the Klingspor foundry in 1927.
The face was named to honor the newly completed
trans-Atlantic telephone cable.
Today the typeface is licensed by the Elsner+Flake GbR foundry.
Kabel stroke weights are more varied
than most geometric sans-serifs, and the terminus of vertical strokes
are cut to a near eight-degree angle.
This has the effect of not quite sitting on the baseline and provides
a more animated, less static feeling than Futura.
The cover title is set in Fletcher Gothic from Casady & Greene.
Fletcher Gothic is an Art Nouveau font with
clean lines and striking details.
The original name of this beautiful Art Nouveau font was
IIRC Toulouse Lautrec, but it became a "famous font"
through the TV series *Murder She Wrote* starring
Angela Lansbury as detective novelist Jessica Fletcher.
Ghosted photo is by C. V. Smith of her bronze sculpture, *Quabbin*.

CPSIA information can be obtained at www.ICGtesting.com
Printed in the USA
265762BV00001B/7/P